A Short Course in Creative Writing

By

Ruby Allure

Copyright Ruby Allure.

For my lovely students

who always astounded me

by the random stories

floating around their minds!

CHAPTER 1

Introduction

What do you want to write? That is the first place to start. It is a simple question; however, there are so many options and so many genres that making this decision is paramount before putting finger to keyboard. One of the best ways to determine precisely what you want to create is to make a mind map. To do this take a piece of paper and write the question 'what do I want to write?' From this little bubble make arrows and boxes, then once you have an arrangement of boxes decide what the priority is by creating a list. At number 1 write your top priority and list the other writings in order.

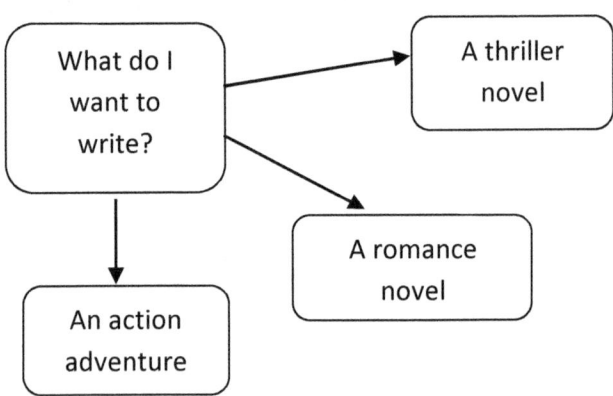

Another way to discover what you wish to create is to free write, which is where you simply write a statement and respond to it by writing as fast as you can without actually consciously thinking. The outcome is often quite a surprise.

With this in mind, I would use the following statement to enable the free-flow:

I want to write…. (this is your prompt) now write as fast as you can until you have nothing left.

Quite often students want to write lots of things and become caught up in all the potentials. They then write nothing because there are too many options. I call this the asteroid syndrome where all the ideas are floating around the students' heads but they remain in space until one lands.

When you complete this prompt notice all the potential pieces that you wish to write then make a priority order in a list. Decide on the first project and then take action. When I say action – I mean begin. As obvious as it seems, to write one has to actually write. Writing is not walking around thinking about it, it is not doing the washing up, the cleaning or phoning a friend. Writing is sitting down and writing.

A few little things to consider about what you wish to write. Writing a memoir or a life story is the opportunity to step into yourself, reflect upon your life and share it with others. This type of writing is based on reality, the experienced, a history and a series of events that have been interpreted by the person whose life it is. Writing a memoir or personal life story is the prime opportunity to re-live, remember, re-experience and possibly even resolve life events. Through writing a memoir or life story not only are you sharing who you are and your experiences, you are enabling yourself a

3

catharsis - a way in which to process events. Through writing your life story you will re-visit situations from a new perspective. You may even notice that you have changed in your approach and perception as you have matured.

Constructing a memoir will involve writing from reality. To gain clarity one may reference old journals, diaries or letters to remind the writer what has taken place. This style of writing is classed as writing from reality because it references actual events, real people and that which has actually taken place. Writing from reality is often known as non-fiction which covers: newspaper stories, editorials, personal accounts, journal articles, textbooks, legal documents and documentary.

Fiction, on the other hand, is imagined; however, it can be built from real life people, places and events. Fiction stories, although constructed from the imagination, are often written to suggest that the story is real. The author often writes the story by researching, imagining and referencing through research. Fiction covers poems, stories, plays, novels, film scripts and dramas.

In addition, fiction is commonly divided into three areas. This division comes from the general appearance of the text:

- Stories and novels are made up of prose usually which follow the usual paragraph structure. The story is then divided into chapters
- Poetry consists of lines of varying length. Sometimes there is rhyme, other times there is simply a rhythm within the construct.
- Plays/scripts consist of spoken lines, stage/television directions. The play is arranged in scenes and acts.

If you think about it, the difference ultimately comes from the mind – the imagined versus the remembered/experienced.

Some of the best advice that I have been given is to write about what you know. The question then becomes what do we really know? Where does reality stop and fiction begin – is there a blur? When we write fiction we often take aspects of what we know, our reality, and combine the realistic ingredients to create a story. There is a fine line between what we remember, our reality and using what we have experienced to generate fictions. With this in mind, have you noticed that you and a friend have different memories of the same event?

Try the following: Write a short piece or journal entry from memory using one of the following titles. Please choose an event or a situation where other people were involved.

- The Biggest Challenge I Overcame
- The Day My Life Changed
- What I Never Expected
- The Reason I Laughed So Hard
- My Most Inspiring Moment
- The Major Event!

Now I would like you to take your reality piece and consider the other people who were involved in the event. Considering who else was involved, step into their shoes and write the event from their point of view. What would they notice? How would they feel? How were they involved?

Now sit and imagine a random character, observe them and make a fiction story from the third person perspective.

- The Ultimate Challenge
- Life Changes
- The Most Unexpected Situation
- A Reason To Laugh
- A Moment Of Inspiration
- A Little Bit Awkward
- Their Major Event.

At this point you will notice that maybe one style of writing is easier. Now we are ready to consider style and voice☺

CHAPTER 2

Ideas and Their Origins

The kiss of inspiration snuck up one evening and kissed you quite unexpectedly. From that moment an idea rattled around your brain like a pea in a can. That idea will constantly niggle you like a child tugging on your trousers. The idea must have expression - that is just how it is.

- The idea is growing. It will convince you that it is definitely original and no one has ever thought of such an amazing idea before. In fact this idea will slowly consume you and compel you to tell everyone about it.
- Great – write it down. An idea is great; however, it is just an asteroid floating around space until gravity captures it and brings it into reality. It then becomes the shooting star!
- Buy yourself a writing journal and keep a scrapbook. Capture everything related to this idea and allow the idea to germinate and grow.
- Before we go any further – does this idea give you a sense of passion? Does it make you want to spend hours developing and refining? Does the thought of spending two hours a day making this idea reality appeal?
- IDEAS-> MASS OF IDEAS-> FILTER-> FINAL IDEA-> BACKGROUND-> CHARACTERS-> THEME-> LOCATION-> STORY-> ERA-> GENRE-> FULL CONCEPT-> WORKING TITLE-> PREPARE TO BEGIN.

The Source of Inspiration

The Art of Noticing

Have you ever considered what you notice and why you notice it?
We all have very different ways of filtering the world around us and each of us approach situations with completely different systems of identification. Take for example a party environment. One person will notice conversations, another will notice body language and maybe another will notice aromas or outfits.

As an interesting exercise write down three things that you notice in any given situation. Once you have listed three usual/obvious items, I suggest you search for three less obvious traits/details. In addition, attempt to notice using different senses. That way you open up your mind to extended noticing.

With what you have noticed consider how you witness the world around you.
Are you primarily visual, auditory or do you notice smells?
Try sharing this idea with a friend and compare what you notice. Is it the same?
What can you learn from how other people notice the world? How can you apply this learning to your writing?
How could you enable an insight into a character through the ways in which they notice?

Story Generation

In a world filled by stories, where do we actually originate inspiration?
Some questions you may wish to consider once you have established what you wish to write:
Why do we want to write it? One needs a 'why' for motivation. Is the 'why' to write your life story for future generations? Is it a burning desire to put on paper a story that has been floating about your mind for years?

Will writing this story provide us with pure enjoyment or enable us to experience life from a different perspective?

How will you reward yourself once you have written this story? Rewarding yourself for completion is something paramount. I ask my students to list a reward, it is usually the following: a spa day, a new handbag, pretty new shoes, track days, adventure day out or a dinner at a nice restaurant. The point of having a reward is to celebrate your success. That way you train yourself to complete what you start.

Back to the story: The truth is that stories are everywhere; it is just a case of noticing them. Some of the more obvious examples come from newspapers, magazines, television, history, myths, fairy tales and our own lives.

With all this in mind, have a look at the below checklist to make sure you have clarity:

- What is it that you wish to write?
- What is the idea?
- What is its theme?
- Why must you share this with the world?
- Who would be interested?
- What are the key components of the idea?
- What can they be linked to?
- What is your intended outcome? – A novel, a short story or an epic?
- What would you like to gain from the journey of writing this?
- What are the emotions involved?
- What research is involved?
- What locations do you need to visit?
- Who could you talk to about the idea?
- Who will give you genuine feedback?
- What is the location? What is the era/timeframe?
- Who are your characters and why do they appeal?
- What is the story really about?
- Why is it that we wish to write the story?
- Who will it appeal to?
- Is it real?
- If it is fiction, does something similar already exist?
- What genre?
- Whose point of view?
- How can I make this unique?
- What can I bring to this that is purely mine?
- What is my reward?

Once we have an idea or a theme – how do we expand and evolve our ideas?

Some of the obvious examples are as follows:

- Brain storms with cards. Write on cards and arrange them into a story.
- Mind map. Draw a diagram and have arrows and boxes leading in all directions.
- Cutting construction. Make cuttings from magazines and use these as prompts.
- Random word prompt. Take a walk, listen out to conversations and use a word that jumps out at you to be your prompt.
- Random theme prompt. It could be love, travel, sport – any theme can prompt you.
- Object story generation. Take two random objects and write a story that links them.
- Open random book/dictionary on a page. Find a theme there.
- Internet idea generator: http://www.seventhsanctum.com/generate.php?Genname=quickstory

Problem Solving as a Story Generator

One of my favourite ways to initiate a story is simply the action of solving a problem. Take for example the following:

- Overhearing a conversation that affects a friend. How do you let them know?
- The craving for a bacon sandwich but having no bacon in the fridge.
- Having to shop for a gift for someone who has everything.
- The need for a cup of sugar when you have moved into a new flat.
- The response to a power cut.
- A problem often initiates a journey. Take for example taking a pregnant friend to hospital.
- Discovering someone jammed in a window.
- Being locked out of your house.
- Being stuck in a lift.

A Random Object as a Story Generator

If in doubt, find a random object and make a story for the object.

Objects often have stories of their own. Who created the object? How did the object come into the possession of the present owner? What is special about the object? By having something real in front of you it becomes easier to stimulate the mind. The Hare With The Amber Eyes is a novel that traces a family's history based on rare objects that were collected by the family.

Filtering Down

Once we begin brainstorming, we soon realise that there is a potential story explosion. If we are not careful we can be consumed by creative chaos. With this in mind, after expanding our creative potential, we now need to structure and narrow down all the ideas. There are a number of techniques for this.

- Lists common themes.
- Colour coding/circling.
- The arrangement of cards which lists the details to generate the structure of the story.

CHAPTER 3

Narrative Voice and Style

The storyteller, who is the narrator, has numerous choices regarding how to narrate their story. It is better that this decision is made early on to stop confusion or constant flitting about throughout the story.

First Person

The first person narrative is one of the most common approaches to narration whereby the author narrates by becoming a character within the story. The plot is revealed by referring to this viewpoint character as 'I'. Usually, the first person narrative is used as a way to provide internal insight and convey the deep internal unspoken thoughts of the narrator. The narrator's story often revolves around themselves as the protagonist. This method allows this protagonist/narrator character's inner thoughts/perspective to be conveyed openly to the audience. It also enables the character to be further developed through his/her style of story telling.

Example: It wasn't as if I could do anything. I sat there helplessly watching Russet, my dog, devour my date's beautiful shoe. I glanced at her sleeping beside me and wondered what else I could give Russet to chew on.

Second Person View

The rarest mode in literature is the second person narrative technique whereby the narrator refers to the reader as 'you'. Using this style of narrative the author makes the reader feel as though he or she is a character within the story. Second person narrative mode is often paired with the first person narrative mode in which the narrator makes emotional comparisons between the thoughts, actions, and feelings of 'you' versus 'I'.

The second-person point of view provides an intense sense of intimacy between the narrator and the reader. That way the reader feels involved but powerless as they are escorted through the plot.

> Example: You are not the kind of person who should be here. So why are you here when you were not invited? You are at this party, so maybe you are here for a reason. You must know why you have chosen this situation. Maybe it is your idea of an accident or a joke. So why do you invade this space? All eyes are on you because something isn't reading right.

Third Person View

Third person narration is the most flexible and the most common approach within literature. I often liken it to an observer standing on a cloud who is able to view all things. In the third person narrative each character is referred to as 'he', 'she', 'it', or 'they'. The third person narrative enables the narrator distance without attachment and makes it obvious that the narrator is an unspecified entity, voice of God or an uninvolved person. That entity narrates the story from an objective or subjective perspective.

Chantelle strolled into the lounge with a look of delight on her face. Admittedly there were hints of what she had been up to decorating her face. She even had pink icing on her cheek and eyebrow.

"I finally managed to achieve my goal!" She exclaimed with joy.

Chantelle had devoured thirteen pink cupcakes in a row without feeling queasy. She was ready for the village cupcake eating championship!

Subjective narrative describes one or more character's feelings and thoughts often in *Italics.*

Objective narration does not describe the feelings or thoughts of any of the characters. Instead, the focus is on the actions. Those actions are 'shown' for the reader to interpret.

An omniscient narrator has knowledge of all times, people, places, and events, including all characters' thoughts.

A limited narrator, in contrast, may know absolutely everything about a single character and every piece of knowledge in that character's mind, but the narrator's knowledge is 'limited' to that character. That is, the narrator cannot describe things unknown to the focal character.

Alternating Person View

The alternating point of view seems to be what often happens when students desire to reveal as much as they can about characters. They often start with first person and then add in a point of view from a new character. This is where the author has to make a definite decision about the approach because the worst thing that can happen is that the author writes the whole book and realises that multiple character viewpoints have become confusing. This is why the general rule for novels is to adopt a single point of view approach throughout a narrative. There are exceptions to this rule and some stories, especially in literature, alternate between the first and third person. This technique enables the author to move back and forth between the God view (with a third-person narrator) to a more personal first person narrator. However, bear in mind your reader and the potential for dis-engagement according to complexity and attention span.

The Stream of Consciousness Narration

This technique is often from a first person point of view. The intention is to provide a narrator's perspective by attempting to replicate the thought process rather than speech or actions of the narrative character. This is where interior monologues, inner desires or motivations and pieces of incomplete thoughts are expressed to the reader. The other characters within the story often remain unaware of these thoughts.

Epistolary Narrative

The epistolary narrative uses a series of letters and other documents to convey the plot of the story. Although epistolary works can be considered multiple-person narratives, they also can be classified separately, as they arguably have no narrator at all, just an author who has gathered the documents together in one place.

A bit of a fun writing break. Have a rest and look at the below prompts:

Write a piece on the following:

- The funniest situation I can remember/imagine
- The most awkward moment
- An act of idiocy

Now look at what you have written. Did you automatically fall into first person or third person? You may have fallen into second person. Which point of view is most natural to you? Once you have written one piece try another one of the prompts using another point of view. Was that easy or more difficult? The reason that you are doing this is to find out your easy way before writing an epic and finding out that maybe you should have written it from a different point of view.

Before writing consider the following:

Who/what is telling the story?

- Me?
- Third person?
- Voice of God?
- Second person?
- A specific character?
- A journalistic - real approach?

With every piece you write it is worth answering the following questions to enable clarity:

- What style?
- What era?
- What is the purpose of what I wish to write?
- What do I wish to learn about?
- What part of me do I wish to explore?
- What makes me special?
- What can I give?
- What do I/character care about?
- Who is my audience?

- What do I want them to experience/feel?
- What do I/or my character want to overcome?
- What are my/my character's motivations?
- What do you want readers to take away from the story?
- What am I specialist in?

The Three States of You and Your Writing

Now this is something worth considering prior to writing your first piece. Which part of you is writing the story? Consider this: we have you at your best, you at your worst and you at your neutral state where you simply get on with it. Obviously there are variations of those states in-between. I had never really considered the difference in my style of writing according to my mood or my state of being. Once I discovered this I purposely began to step into the state of me at my best where I considered how I would inspire and uplift through writing. When I was in my worst state, I tried writing from this point of view, writing was like mud and the writing landscape became murky. It was fascinating because even writing like that became a chore. The neutral state of writing was simply a case of not gauging a mood and writing simply to write. There is nothing wrong with this state of writing; however, the writing that I produced in my 'best state' was quite beautiful in comparison to the other versions. Again this relates to writing to heal and catharsis. Try writing in your three states:

When I write at my best I am… and I feel….
When I write in my neutral state I am and I feel…
When I write in my worst state… I am and I feel.

Have a read of the three pieces of writing and notice the wording you use. Is there a difference? So with this in mind, pick one of the below prompts and see what you do with them according to the state you choose:

What caught my attention about him/her was…. (write from each state).
The situation I found myself in resulted in….
When I was handed the key I instantly thought…

BEFORE WE GO ANY FURTHER – Notice the voices in your head. Listen to what they are saying. Is one of them being negative and saying "Why are you doing this? It is just a waste of time? I will never be good enough?"
If so you are really not alone. One of the biggest struggles I witness with my students is that the inner critic comes out when they are being creative. It gains power when they are about to read out their work too. There are many ways to deal with the inner critic, however, I have learned to thank it when it starts chatting. It is there for a reason – it tries to stop you feeling ridiculed or stupid. So, it kindly sets you up to fail before you have even started. Now not only do you have an inner critic, there is also an inner coach. The coach will be excited about all the possibilities to write. When you start feeling not good enough and the critic is rife, switch to the inner coach. Listen to all the positive aspects you are experiencing through writing.

Another huge thing that I have noticed is that when the students become overwhelmed by the inner critic, they delete huge sections of good writing. So with this in mind, always write in version 1. This is your first draft and keep writing it until it is complete. It will not be perfect, no one can ever write a perfect draft – fact! So write your story or book until complete. Save it as version 1 and every time you edit, save it as the next version, 2,3,4 however many. That means that your first draft is never lost and good writing will never disappear.

CHAPTER 4

Character Construction and Consideration.

Characters are the crucial to the writing of excellent fiction and non-fiction. Characters who are dull, two dimensional and lifeless do not engage the reader, that is, unless there is purpose behind the dullness or lifelessness. Readers are usually fascinated by quirks, mystery and curiosity. A level of identification is also useful to enable identification with the character. One of the easiest ways to create an interesting character is to create a biography (a character history) of that character. You may like to consider the following when building your character:

Note: you can use these considerations for real or imagined characters.

- Attitude
- Posture
- Tattoos
- Accent
- Origin
- Gender
- History
- Wealth
- Religion
- Height
- Build
- Job/career
- Addictions – drinking, smoking, coffee, sex or food?

- Hairstyle
- What activities do they do?
- How do they maintain themselves?
- What is their choice of clothing?
- What period of time were they born?
- What do they eat? What is their favourite food?
- What are their ambitions?
- What motivates them?
- Who are their friends?
- Have they made any sacrifices?
- Have they suffered hard times?
- What makes them who they are?
- Who would they like to be?
- Where do they go on holiday?
- How do they cope with stress?
- What makes them stressed?
- Do they exercise? What sort of exercise?
- Inner world/outer world.
- What kind of house do they live in?
- Are they single or married?
- Do they have children?
- Do they suffer from any ailments?
- Victim, rescuer or persecutor?
- Why are they interesting?
- Are they overweight or underweight?
- Why would anyone want to read about them?
- What are their fears?
- What is the worst situation you could put them in?

- If they had to confess one thing what would they confess?
- What are their quirks?
- Do they fall into a stereo type or cliché?
- What are their flaws?
- What are their hobbies?
- Satisfaction level – happy and content versus angry and discontent?
- What would their friends say about them?
- What would their mum say about them?
- How do they justify their behaviour?
- What makes them laugh?

Consider the below approaches:

1) Sometimes it is easier to find a picture that resembles the character you intend to create. Try browsing through art books that feature portraits. Family photos, magazines and the Internet are great resources for finding inspiring faces.

2) When writing about the character consider all the senses. How do they appear? What stands out? How does the person talk? Accent, tone of voice, stutter? What smells come to mind? What aftershave or perfume would they choose? How would you describe their skin, hair, clothes and posture?

3) Consider the people around you including friends, relatives and co-workers. When you write what you know it is more convincing. Real life is often more interesting than the imagined. Using what you know, try combining character traits of those who you like and dislike.

4) An individual exists beyond the moment and so should your character. Build the personality outside the story. Consider their past, present and future. Accumulate as many details as possible until you really know that person. Consider them in different situations, on a train, in a lift, at a party or dealing with a crisis.

5) Look at the inner traits of the character versus how they are appear. What the character conceals makes them interesting too. What is the character's inner dialogue? What is the character trying to conceal from the world?

All of the above will help you develop a more three dimensional character.

6) A basic character sketch can include:

- Physical description
- Career
- Partner/Ideal partner
- What makes them angry and what makes them happy
- Strengths and weaknesses
- Hobbies
- Fears & Hopes
- History

- Family
- Dreams
- Quirks
- Attributes

7) Consider using metaphors and do your best to avoid stereotypes. The most vicious bully could be in the guise of the sweetest little girl instead of the more obvious bulldog-featured man. Also the character who is willowy can be considered metaphoric for flexibility and lenience. The rigid character can be considered stubborn or resistant.

8) It is often the case that the best loved characters have the most obvious flaws. A character with flaws, quirks and emotions is far more interesting than those who are perfect. Consider positive and negative traits. The villain who evokes sympathy because of their flaws is far more powerful and interesting than someone who is simply vile and rotten to the core. Imagine a character who desperately wants to be kind but when the kindness is not noticed they become angry.

9) Avoid being too obvious. It is all very easy to re-create characters that we have been influenced by; however, the fun is pushing them and making them more interesting.

10) The general consensus of opinion is that perfect characters are not that interesting. So have fun using contradictions and polarities. Take for example the cleaner who does not wash or the gourmet chef who lives on fast food.

EXERCISE FOR CHARACTERS:

Write two positive traits such as kindness and compassion. Now write one negative trait such as anger or jealousy. Use these traits to describe one of the characters you have in mind.

To make the characters more complex write three positive traits like cheerful, optimistic and gentle with two negative traits such as a compulsive liar and manipulator. Take these to a character you have in mind and write the character with these traits. See what happens and where your character leads you.

CHAPTER 5

The Triad of Change

The triad is a technique that can be applied to how we work with creative writing.

This is a model that enables you to find your 'easy way' to write because we don't all work in the same way. It will enable you to ascertain your best approach for creative writing and how to build your books.

Finding an easy way to create stops the struggle and makes the creative process enjoyable.

There are two ways to live life:

- The hard way – where it will always be painful.
- The easy way – where effort turns into progress.

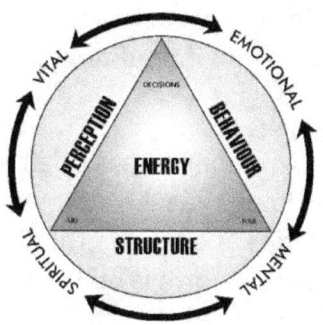

Think of a time where you have triumphed with writing or any goal in life. Now consider how you approached this goal and what made you determined. To succeed you must have used a success strategy – one that worked for you. It was the way in which you approached the situation that produced a desired outcome. Progress comes from using the correct strategy.

COMPONENTS

Perception

When we think about an idea, until we have it clear in our heads, we use perception as a strategy. Using the car analogy, a person thinks about the destination, the journey and imagines it all without actually going on the journey or stepping into the car. The journey is simply an idea.

Perception is a point of view or an opinion to make change. Those with perception need to understand why something is important to bring it into reality. To make the idea real take the perceived story into vision or meditation and holding the image in your mind imagine it written on paper, that way the outcome you intend to produce will be effective.

In terms of writing, this approach is originating the idea in your head and imagining the whole picture. I would describe this as a series of clouds gathering to generate a writing storm! Once the storm is built, make the thunder and lightning manifest in reality. Often the perceptive types get very caught up in the dream and then the next dream because it is so much fun imagining. The challenge is for the perceptive sorts to action what they imagine. So they have to have bursts of writing to get the ideas onto paper. This is why you need to determine why your project is important to make real.

Structure

When we take the pieces of what we intend to do and build a framework we are using structure. We assemble the 'building blocks' of what we wish to create and then know our order and fill out the details. This approach is structural and quite often appears in lists or flow diagrams. In terms of going on a journey in a car, this person details every part of the route and lists precisely the turnings and points of interest before commencing the journey.

Structure contains supports and organizes the existence of something or gives something existence. It organises time and space. It can also be a financial plan, a map, a list, a policy or a fitness regime.

In terms of creative writing – the author will organise their book and create an order. They will then fit the story to that order. The best way for this type to write is daily and with discipline. If they have an allotted time and routine then they will happily write regularly until they complete their masterpiece. When their time is structured the writing becomes easy.

Behaviour

Sometimes people just get on with what they need to do – they just do it. This is the behaviour strategy. As they work through what they are doing they simply add, adjust or re-order until it is complete. Once their project is complete they get on with it and re-order it. It would be the same as climbing in a car and simply driving without knowing the route or the destination.

Behaviour is action taken to effect change or create. This may involve physical effort or movement, involve an energy or an action that takes you into something new. The repeated behaviour drives you towards your goal.

In terms of writing, this behaviour is simply about the act of writing. You simply write and then build the parts you have written into a structure afterwards. These people aren't willing to sit around talking or thinking or ordering... they will just get on with it and finish it and then get on with the next one.

Questions to ask your writing self:

What comes most easily to you?

Structure, behaviour or perception? What technique has resulted in success in the past? Which style has caused you to miss out? What way do you find easiest to write? If you are thinking about this for a while you are probably perception based. The behavioural person would have just started writing or skipped through the chapters and the structure will be mapping how they best worked previously and probably finding evidence.

- The truth is when you are in a state of creativity you connect to something deeper within yourself. You can label this however you like.

Consider what society has taught us-to push against that which does not work and to improve our weakness – why? In my opinion why focus on your weaknesses when you can use your strength? If you have an easy way to achieve something then use it. There is far too much energy wasted on that which does not work. Essentially what does not work does not matter. Also if you feel you are constantly battling then you will find procrastination increases. The whole point of creative writing is to enjoy it and not struggle.

THE KICKER: Often what you think you are good at is sometimes your weakness.

Strengths and How to Use Them

LEADING WITH BEHAVIOUR

- Get on and do it
- Take action now
- Get right on with it – start working on a project-no waiting around. Waiting and thinking makes you feel at a loss
- Jump in – think later – impulsive...
- Once you have the picture – make the plan.

For you to feel better change what you are doing, get started or do an exercise – it will inspire. Just do something different.

BEHAVIOUR PEOPLE take immediate action. If something is not working then change what you are doing. Your motto is 'Just do it.' When you need to think or find a new way do something physical right where you are.

When overwhelmed with too much to do then make a list and cross off.

Get started on anything.

Sometimes to feel alive you just need to do something different – anything.

For progress in place of pain – stop-ask what is going on and what do you need to 'do?'

LEADING WITH STRUCTURE:

- This is the framework.
- Need to get things in order.
- Clean and organise.
- The picture is lost unless the steps are there.
- Putting things in order is helpful.
- Ready, fire, aim. This is how the structure person works – they need to know how it is built rather than just do it. They need the elements to build.
- Plan it – even if the plan changes. The enjoyment can be in re-arranging the plan.

NOTE: When things are not going your way, stop and do something that physically changes structure, like re-arrange something. Touch your toes. Re-organise. Get out of the building or room. Make a plan to solve something. Take apart an object and re-arrange it. Change a plan. It can be simple but it has to be located in a time and space. Make a schedule and slot things into an agenda. How will I prioritise things to get them done in time?

LEADING WITH PERCEPTION:

The perception person:

- Needs a picture – why does this need to happen?
- There needs to be a meaning to enable action to be taken
- To progress it is best that you visualise, feel or talk about an objective
- Perspective guides your actions and plans
- Questions – what am I happy about? What sucks?
- If I can imagine... then I can make it real

NOTE: Know what you want or where you want to be... Visualise it and get it clear in your head. Know your why and then make it happen. This applies to change too.

THE BIG QUESTIONS:

This triad can be applied to more than just writing. If you are interested in how to use this triad to make change then try the following as a writing exercise:

Remind yourself – what are the four things (in one sentence) that you need to do to change a situation.

What four things do you need to bring to your writing to make you feel good?

Attitude and the way we look at things makes a huge difference in one's life.

Questions to ask to help you organise yourself to realise which is easier:

What behaviours work for me?

What is it that makes me feel good?

What is it that I can structure?

What do I like structuring?

How do I structure?

What perception works?

What do I need to imagine?

How do I imagine this will feel when I complete this work and what does it look like?

How can I use my lead strategy?

CHAPTER 6

What?

Now we have found our easy way of doing things then... So what? We have created a number of characters and made a few biographies. Now what are we going to do with them? And what ordeals do we want them to experience? You have already decided what you want to write but is it:-

- A short story
- An article
- A novel
- A full novel
- Fiction
- Autobiography
- Biography
- A treatment
- A sales pitch
- A poem

There are so many potential outcomes with what you could write. Once we have decided what we want to write we then have to choose our voice and point of view.

Voice:

- Formal
- Informal
- Third person
- Point of view

- Multiple person
- Diary

Who/what is telling the story?

- Me
- Third person
- Voice of God
- A character
- A journalistic-real approach

Then there are the following questions:

- What style?
- What era
- What is the purpose of what I wish to write
- What do I wish to learn about
- What part of me do I wish to explore
- What makes me special
- What can I give
- What do I/character care about
- Who is my audience
- What do I want them to experience/feel
- What do I/or my character want to overcome
- What are my/my character's motivations
- What do you want readers to take away from the story
- What am I specialist in

This part is very interesting because you suddenly realise you are specialist in many things that you can share with the world. Take for example people who drink wine – they may have an interest in South African wine. You may have an interest in cake baking. You may work in finance so therefore spend your time watching money. Someone may have lost a large amount of weight – they can share this. We may go on interesting holidays – you become a specialist on coach trips or cruises. We all have interests, we are all specialists in something. It is just knowing what your specialist is. List everything you have an interest in or have experienced. This is your unique contribution, even if it was taking part in gymnastics at the age of nine or planting strawberries in your garden. This is all part of your uniqueness.

What do I know?

FREE WRITE:

I know about_____ which I can turn into a_____

I feel passionate about_____ that I can turn into_____.

My favourite subject to write about is_____ which I can turn into_____.

What genre?

Fiction:

- Fantasy
- Literary
- Chick lit
- Travel story
- Romance

Is it true life?

- A diary
- An autobiography
- A biography
- History
- Military history
- Self-help
- Medical
- Travel

Whose story is it?

What is the theme?

What setbacks do I want the character to encounter?

What is the climax?

What can I make the character confront or experience?

What are the most exciting situations/experiences that I can create within this writing?

What ignites my creativity?

BRAIN STORM / FREE WRITE:

If you could describe what you wish to write about in one sentence....

If there were no limits what would you 'love' to create?

The Story/Article/Biography

What is the story?

Whose story is it?

Who is telling it?

What is the theme?

What is the research?

What planning do I need to do?

What can I write backwards? – Meaning what do I want to achieve as the ultimate goal – how do I get there?

What do I believe about the story?

What do I want to believe about the story?

What gives me a gut reaction?

MORE FREE WRITING:

What I wish to create is....

FILL IN THE GAPS:

The story is about_____ who
wants to_____ and ends
up_____ and the emotions felt
are_____ which results
in_____ with the final
outcome_____.

The article is about_____ and will
appeal to_____.

I intend to provide information specifically
on_____ which has been researched
from/ has been based on_____
. My reader will come away with_____ .
They will learn_____ and
will gain insight on_____.

What Routine?

Now that you have defined your 'whats' then it is time to begin writing. The easiest way to write, in my opinion, is to allocate a specific time per day and write. Whether it is good writing or terrible – the point is you start a routine. It is like Pavlov's dogs, where you won't exactly salivate, well you may do mentally, but your mind will expect to write at a certain time and will respond accordingly. That way if you set yourself a target of one thousand words per day then in a month you would have drafted a novelette or in two months you would have the word count for a small novel. Obviously you can write in stints; however, I view writing as exercise. When you train daily and regularly you maintain fitness. Spurts of exercise only result in injury!

THE ENEMY: PROCRASTINATION!

Don't think about it – just do it. Meaning sit and write, don't think about writing – instead simply sit down and get on with it... As much as tidying, phone calls or dusting may be calling – sit down and write. If nothing comes – mind map and work on character design or plot. Just get something on paper! My students have provided me with great amusement over the years with their excuses of why they didn't write and what they did to distract themselves. Yes it is funny that someone used a toothbrush to clean between their tiles for two hours rather than write. The worst excuse ever is worming the dog. However, no one is forcing anyone to write. It is a pleasure and a gift. When you find yourself procrastinating become aware of the inner saboteur. They are great friends with the inner critic.

They will do what they can to dissuade you so that you fail. The reason they do this is because if you change and succeed that means your whole life will change because then anything you put your mind to becomes possible. If everything is possible then what have you been doing all this time? Answer: giving the saboteur and critic power.

KEY TIP ON WRITING FOREVER:

A hint is to create an ideas file. Capture articles and snippets of notes that you can refer to later. Anything that is of interest whether it is visual or written. Oh and make sure you maintain that writing journal too.

FINALLY: WHAT WILL MAKE YOUR CREATION MORE ENJOYABLE?

Is it making the writing juicier? Or is it changing the voice? Is it the research?

What will make this piece of work the most fun/enjoyable/special/unique piece of writing that you have ever created?

CHAPTER 7

Imagining, Sensing and Writing about a Location

To transport your writer into a world that you have created requires the ability to evoke engaging mental imagery. One of the joys of portraying a location/scene is the prospect of creating a three dimensional description with a sense of the locations 'personality'. Take for example a room, you can reveal a great deal about a person by the design of a room and what is kept within the room. Ornaments and objects of sentimentality are often quite revealing.

As with all aspects of your writing, there are numerous considerations:

- Are you approaching the location writing from a journalistic or a creative point of view?
- What is the purpose of the location?
- Does the location further the story?
- Is the location to be referenced as part of an article?
- Is the location the central focus of an article?
- What is unique in your approach?
- If the writing is referencing fiction, how do different characters view the same location?

Sequence

When writing about a location, whether it's from a character's point of view, a documentary or from the first person point of view, there will usually be a sequence of noticing. Take for example when you first visit a house you would first notice where you park, the road you are parked on then maybe the gate, a path, the garden, the porch, the door, the letter box, the hallway, the front room/lounge, the décor and then the details of the ornaments. Since we all notice in different ways, create your own sequential order. Alternatively the order of noticing can be purposely used to reveal a character or purposely disorientate the reader.

The description of a location provides the perfect opportunity to direct the attention of your reader/audience. The interior of a house may well be a complete contrast to the exterior. Take for example a cream tea cottage set amongst fields having an ultra-modern interior. What does that reveal? What I will say is that there is a real joy of choosing what to describe within a location. Many writers use the location or house to reveal the intricacies of the character.

With all the above in mind, when describing a location consider the following:

- Where is the location?
- What era is the location?
- When you walk into the location, what does it 'feel like?'
- What does the location remind you of?
- What emotions have been felt there?
- Whose point of view are we seeing the location from?
- What colour is it?
- What time of day is it?
- How is the room lit?
- What are the walls like? Are there walls?
- What details do you notice?
- Are there ornaments? What are they like?
- What style is the furniture?
- Is there furniture?
- How would a child respond to the room?
- How would a builder view the room?
- How would your character view the room?
- What is the temperature of the room?
- How can you conjure an image easily of the room?
- Is there a theme?
- What is special about the room?
- Is it clean?
- Is there dust?
- Are there mirrors?
- Is there a design to the room?

- Is it sparse?

Once you have painted the picture in your mind, consider what is relevant about the room. How would Sherlock Holmes link the details of the room?

Where in the room would you stand? Where in the room are you viewing the room from? If you viewed the room from a different position, how would it change?

How would your mother or mother-in-law perceive the room? What comments would she make?

When writing about locations there are three main approaches that I use:

- The imagined/remembered
- Picture stimulation
- Write on location

The most interesting thing to notice is how the descriptions differ depending on which technique you choose. When you have read through the work select the most effective way for you. Alternatively you may notice that all techniques have strengths and wish to use a combination of all three. Since your ultimate goal is to be as convincing as possible, choose the technique which will enable the most clarity and provide the most engaging/insightful writing (if that is what you desire).

NOTE: Be careful of over description – do not bore the reader with dull details. I don't know about you but I have read books that have provided rambling, dull descriptions which made me put the book down. Attempt to find fun and interesting ways to portray a room. Read the description aloud. Ask yourself does the writing provide the vision/paint the picture and reveal what you intend it to reveal? Can you make it better? How?

Finally….

Collect information about locations that inspire you - whether it is travel articles, architecture magazines or interiors. That way you will always have reference material to step into when you need a hint of writing inspiration.

CHAPTER 8

The Delights of Dialogue

How an individual speaks and gestures reveals a great deal about them. From a simple conversation we can discover an individual's perspective, mood and thoughts. How that person converses has been developed over their whole lives and is a result of their experience, upbringing, core beliefs/backstory/history.

Notice the following when listening to a conversation:

- Origin
- Current fixation/focus
- Levels of intelligence
- Confidence/lack of confidence.
- Articulation.
- Emotion.
- Accent.

People reveal a great deal about what they say through words, body language and what they hold back.

In terms of dialogue, we primarily are interested in getting to know the character. We gauge this through their behaviour, their action and how they speak. Dialogue is used as a tool to drive the story forwards and provides a clearer insight into the character's beliefs/perspective/backstory. What's more, dialogue can be used to deepen and reveal a character's emotion.

You will also find that the inner world will result in the way in which the character communicates.

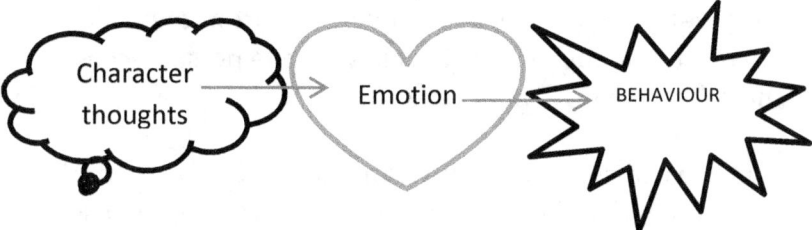

Prior to writing a character's dialogue, ask yourself the following:

- What mood is the character in?
- What events have led them to that moment?
- What do they intend to reveal about themselves?
- What is their body language saying?
- What is their perspective on life?
- What are they trying to say, learn or gain?

Write a scene where one person is listening to two other people have an argument or discussion. For example, a child listening to parents argue about money. Have the third character narrate the argument and explain what is going on, but have the other two provide the entire dialog. NOTE: It is not necessary to have the narrator understand the argument completely.

Write a conversation between two liars. Give everything they say a double or triple meaning. Never state or indicate through outside description that these two people are lying. Let the reader figure it out strictly from the dialog. Try not to be obvious, such as having one person accuse the other of lying. That is too easy.

Finally write a character entering the same 'awkward' situation in two different moods. The first one is a positive mood (choose your own emotion). The second time the character enters the situation they are in a very negative mood (again choose the emotion). Notice how they will choose very different words according to the emotion.

Be careful of overusing modifiers – said, whispered, demanded, as examples. It is possible to write dialogue without adding modifiers constantly. Too many dialog modifiers such as shouted, exclaimed, cried, whispered, stammered, opined, insinuated, hedged and a million others become repetitious. Modifiers such as this can sometimes be useful, but are often annoying and used as a crutch for poorly designed dialogue.

"Jack, are you sure?" Jenny asked.

"Yeah, I'm sure."

"Really?"

"Yes, really."

EXAMPLE:

"Jack, I don't get it," Jenny said.

Jack raised an eyebrow. "Don't get what?"

"His behaviour. It doesn't make any sense."

"What isn't there to get? He got angry when she wiped their shared account. Now he wants a divorce."

EXERCISE:

Write the dialog for a scene without using any modifiers. Just write down a conversation as it goes along naturally. After you have completed the dialog, add narrative description, but not dialog tags such as said, shouted or ordered. Instead, try to work the dialog into the action as a logical progression of the statements. Finally, add any dialog tags that are absolutely necessary, and keep them simple such as said, told, or asked. Again, only put them in if you cannot find any other options. Compare this to the previous dialog you have written and see what you like or dislike about the changes.

It is good to break up your dialogue with action so that you can remind your reader that the characters are physical human beings. The action breaks up the dialogue and reveals more about what is happening.

What is that?" She peered into the box, and screamed, "Oh, my God!"

Or "What is that?" She peered into the box. "Oh, my God!"

NOTE: it should be obvious from the dialogue how she is speaking.

One of the best ways to really understand dialogue is to make polarities converse.

Consider playing with the following characters in conversation:

- A prisoner chatting to a nun/monk
- A top athlete talking to someone who is obese
- An optimist talking to a depressive/hypochondriac
- A successful businessman talking to someone who avoids work
- An intellect talking to an idiot
- A bimbo talking to a highly articulate business woman
- A pilot talking to someone with a fear of flying
- A contortionist talking to someone who is rigid and inflexible
- A Namibian goat farmer and an oil-rich billionaire

Consider the following locations for conversation:

- On the train.
- On a bus.
- A new job.

- At a party.
- At a dinner party.
- In a lift.
- On holiday.
- In an interview (media/university/job).
- At a meeting.
- At a wedding.
- At a reception desk of a hotel.
- A waiting room.
- Joining a new club.
- At a bar.
- In a gym changing room/at a gym class.
- School event/parents evening/theatre.
- Speed dating/date.
- Yoga retreat/health spa.
- Diet/alcohol/step programme.
- Sweat lodge.
- A crisis.
- A maternity room.

All of the above locations lend themselves for the perfect opportunity to take part in a conversation/create interesting dialogue. However, when we initially meet we edit what we want people to know about us. We don't confess our inner-most truths straight away, if at all.

Please note: when considering how people speak, listen to conversations, consider the tone of the voice, the accent and the subject. You will be amazed by how much inane chatter there is. An interesting experiment is to listen to a conversation behind you and attempt to guess what the person looks like according to what they are discussing. The majority of the time they will be completely different.

Finally, when entering into conversation start to be aware of body language. The subtle language at work reveals far more about what the person really thinks. Take for example someone nodding with folded arms. Often when someone is telling lies, they touch their nose, avoid eye contact or cover their mouths. All of this reveals an insight into the character.

CHAPTER 9

Show and Not Tell

- The aroma of roses filled the air while a warm breeze ruffled her fringe as she gazed down at the turquoise pool. She took a deep breath and dived in.
- Or..... She jumped in a swimming pool surrounded by roses.
- Hysterical laughter filled the air. People were drunk on the skillful delivery of the comedians' one liners.
- Or.... a comedian made the room laugh.

The point of 'showing' is to paint literary images using words. The reader must use their imagination to build their own virtual world stimulated by the writer's chosen words. The goal is not to overload the reader with literary flounce or heavy-handed adjectives, but rather to allow readers to experience the author's vision by interpreting inter-linked suggestive/evocative vocabulary.

In addition, showing is about demonstrating an action with literary skill. Consider what a character actually does rather than state why. When someone is angry, shifty, excited what happens? What are their actions? What happens and what does the character actually do?

To enable effective showing the author/writer must have absolute clarity of what he or she is describing. In terms of a character, that character must have been built and made real to enable effective show of the character. In terms of location, the same clarity must be applied. When the author/writer has achieved such mental clarity something within the unconscious paints the image between the words. That is when the true mastery is revealed.

When the author knows enough about what they are writing then they may omit specific details to provide enough space for the reader to link the literary jigsaw pieces in their mind. This is a skill and a talent which can only take place once the author/writer is able to visualise the story landscape in absolute clarity.

The unfortunate truth about telling is that it easily becomes habit because telling carries the narrative along quickly. 'She fancied him,' provides a very quick insight. However the joy is discovering the response the character has when they fancy someone.

The flush of rouge climbed from her chest to her chin. Her voice cracked and that was it. It was as if a switch flipped, words of utter nonsense flew from her mouth. She searched frantically for her opportunity to exit. All the while her mouth continued to spew non-sensical sentences.

EXERCISE: Re-write the three 'tells' below in a 'showing' state :

- She fancied him
- They were excited
- He felt angry

Write two sentences and swap them with a partner. Both re-write according to showing and not telling.

Defining Moments in Character

There are many moments in an individual's life where a choice is presented that will change the course of that individual's life 'journey'. This is the same with our characters. When developing a character's backstory it is important to completely understand your character's behaviour. A grown-up who spent their childhood in an unstable home will behave in a very different manner to an adult who has been nurtured. A person who has been through a series of abusive relationships will react very differently to someone who fell in love with their childhood sweetheart and lived in contented bliss. Consider the difference in attitude between two people – one who has stared death in the face and another who has never experienced any loss. All of these are defining moments in a character and the individual.

Often a character's reaction or response is based on a series of learned behaviours that have worked previously. Consider the 'victim' who will adopt victim behaviour to gain sympathy and attention. At some point this behaviour became their survival mode. There was a defining moment where the victim had the choice to become the victim or fight back.

Consider the 'persecutor' who will erupt into rage and be aggressive to 'steal fire'. They erupt in anger, emotionally vomit or make accusations which are often unfounded.

What about the rescuer who feels it is their duty to save and fix others?

All of these behaviours have been learned and they often come from defining moments in an individual's life.

With all this in mind, the reader will be intrigued and attempt to decipher what makes the character behave the way that they do. In everyone's life/back-story there are 'defining' moments. It might be as simple as asking a person on a date. The series of events may result in marriage. If that request had not taken place – would there be regret? Each decision/choice results in action based on internal beliefs and history – one defining moment can alter the course of a personal/character history.

Defining moments, according to 'hero metamorphosis,' are part of the strengthening process. The learning strengthens the hero until they reach a point where they, the 'hero' are ready to step into the chrysalis and completely transform into the proverbial heroic butterfly.

The classic defining moments include:

- A small child facing the school bully.

The defining moment will result numerous outcomes however there are two obvious outcomes - the small child running away or being courageous enough to fight back.

With this in mind, what if this child runs away? Will they always run away? Would there be regret or would there be a sense of relief regarding escape? Your character's traits and temperament will determine how they feel about their response.

Now imagine that same small child punches the bully on the nose. It is very much a David and Goliath situation. The small person overcomes the bully which could result in the bully being humiliated or causing the bully to attempt revenge for the humiliation.

- The relationship break-up.

Relationship break-ups often throw individuals into crisis. There was a recent article on a young woman who experienced a relationship break up and because she could not control the situation she shifted her need to control into another part of life and developed obsessive compulsive disorder.

Others use the break-up to experience new found freedom while others may become obsessed stalkers. It all depends on how your character responds to this defining moment, again based on their traits, values and beliefs.

- Illness

Illness is often a catalyst for change or a wake-up call. The way a character experiences the illness can result in a newly developed health regime or a completely different attitude to life. This 'scare' provides a new perspective and attitude.

- Death

Death of a loved one or relative often makes people reflect on the transience of existence. Death often stimulates life re-evaluation. In terms of characters, the death of a loved one is often the motivation for revenge or a journey.

EXERCISE: Now consider three defining moments in your character. Write a short piece about the defining moment and include the below in the description.

- What was the character's age?
- How did these defining moments affect their life?
- What behaviours do they develop?
- What beliefs have come from the experience?
- What is their attitude to life because of these moments?
- What would have happened if they had made another choice?
- How do they feel about the situation?
- What emotions do they suppress/express?
- How will these affect the narrative?
- How has their life changed because of that moment?

You might want to use this as catharsis for yourself. If so, pick three defining moments and write about them. Once you have completed them now write the defining moment changing according to you picking an alternative outcome. If you really want to go into this then, if another person was involved, write the situation from their point of view and their choice. It is fascinating what comes from this.

Description, Events and Portrayal

List three events that come to mind straight away... Yes three events, whether it is in your own life or in your fiction writing. Tell your potential readers about each event. Write really fast....

- What were your first impressions?
- What was taking place?
- Who was involved?
- What made you think of the event?
- What emotions were involved?
- When did this happen?
- What was the cause and effect?

Now look at what you have written? How much of these events have been clearly described? How would a reader piece together the pictures inside your head?

This is where the art of description comes in for both reality writing and fiction. Your aim is to portray a scene or event with absolute clarity. How do you do this? Consider how you choose to combine words and utlilise words that stimulate the senses. The skill comes from being able to take what is inside your mind and conjure your mental picture through word usage in your reader's mind. The portrayal of a three dimensional scene/person takes skill, however, there are some tried and tested techniques: Consider the senses:

- Smell
- Touch

- Seeing
- Hearing
- Feeling
- Taste

Which of the senses have you used in your descriptions?

Now consider three perceptions from the senses and combine them to enable description. If you wish to intensify description also consider the below:

- An action
- An outcome
- What has been said
- A gesture
- An experience
- Atmosphere
- Repercussion

As an example we could have smell + atmosphere + feeling.

Or we could have what is seen + what is felt + with an action. We take these aspects and bring them into one sentence.

Consider using an aroma combined with an atmosphere and a hint of the location to paint a picture of a time and place where an event is taking place.

- The pungent smell of chlorine violated the burning summer evening in the forest.

An aroma, combined with feeling and an experience.

- The smell of freshly squeezed lemons complimented the cool feeling of freshly mown grass against bare legs.

Consider combining a feeling, an action and a repercussion.

- The redness of her rising rage made her lash out. "It is easy for you!" she scathed!
- The sense of joy made her spine arch backward as she gazed towards the heavens and grinned.

Obviously there are all manner of combinations that one can use. Bear in mind the author always has the choice whether to make a literary sketch for the reader to fill in or a multi-sensory masterpiece that provides clarity and detail. However the author chooses to proceed, the greater the clarity that the author has then the more intensive engagement the reader is provided with.

Aim to transport the reader into a multi-sensory landscape using precise words which evoke emotion, smells and image. The crafting of the language and description enables the reader to stroll through a narrative journey with clarity and a clear mental image that they will remember.

Within your writing there are many details to describe; however, not everything needs a mass of intricacy. Details can be hinted at and precision word usage is a more efficient way of providing description rather than arduous waffle.

The question then becomes what do we describe and what do we leave out? This is up to you.

As a rule of thumb, the main aspects we describe come from the focus of our main character or the person providing the point of view. I look at description metaphorically - as where we shine our torch. If we were shinning our torch in a room what would make us stop waving the torch and pay attention to what was in the light? What is it that draws our focus? Bear in mind the details we notice when we meet a person, enter a location or discover an object. Take for example noticing jewellery on a woman at a gallery showing:

- The pendulous jewellery hung around her neck like a cannon ball on a string.

Imagine walking into a room filled with people chatting.

- The hum of mass murmur filled the air with meaningless chatter while the verbal bees careered into the walls of vast oak panelled hall.

The fun is crafting the sentences with words that may not usually sit with each other.

With all the above in mind, now re-write your three chosen events in such a way that it becomes three-dimensional.

CHAPTER 10

Story and Structure

Essentially a story is a series of linked events that relate to each other. The structure of the story is the result of the assembly of the building blocks. Your intention is to construct a coherent series of events, which a reader can relate to. Without the structure, you simply have a pile of literary bricks. With narrative structure, the beauty of the architecture can attain its full potential. Essentially you are making order from chaos.

Consider the below ingredients for the story:

- Character/hero
- Anti-hero/antagonist
- Location
- Events
- Crisis
- Emotions
- Connections
- Response to events
- Climax
- Interaction between other characters
- Obstacles to overcome
- Love interests
- Goals
- Motivations
- Experience outside of comfort zones
- Transformation of character

- Learning/outcome
- What can be shared with society/the world. Will it be accepted?

Now if you put the above list in a pile, you simply have a meaningless list of labels. Unless the individual parts of the list are inter-related/linked, there is no coherent story. This is where the creativity begins. Using the above list, make a mind map and begin to originate a story world.

Bear in mind that a story introduces a problem and finds a resolution. Often the journey is the learning involved in finding the resolution.

More simply put - a story, script or article usually follows a three act structure. Here are a number of similar approaches to the three act structure:

- Act I-> Act II->Act III.
- Beginning ->Middle->End. (Aristotle)
- Problem->Catalyst and journey->Resolution.
- Emotional problem->Caused by two conflicting emotions->resolution (Foster Harris).

The three act structure is classic, it applies to most plays, stories and films. As with all rules, they are in place to keep you safe, maybe you do not need to follow them, but it is good to be aware of them. That way you can actively choose to break them.

Gustav Freytag approaches structure with the following:

- Exposition->Rising Action->Climax->Falling Action->Resolution.

STORY & PLOT

According to Aristotle, the story tells of a change in fortune that happens to a character. These are usually divided into two.

From good fortune to bad or bad to good.

According to Monomyth, by Joseph Campbell, there is a basic pattern to the majority of narratives around the word. The Monomyth is also referred to as the hero's journey.

You may notice that you naturally bring this into your own work:

DEPARTURE

- Call to action. *Hero begins in the mundane and something triggers a change.*
- Refusal of the call. *There is reason for refusal – attachments, fear, sense of duty.*
- Supernatural aid. *Once committed to the quest an advisor/mentor/ wise person arrives.*
- The crossing of the first threshold. *The beginnings of adventure and a departure from the comfort zone of known limits.*
- Belly of the whale. *This is the final separation of the hero from the life they knew.*

INITIATION

- The Road of Trials. *Bring in the obstacles which will enable failure and learning.*
- The Meeting with the Goddess. *The experience of true love with power and consequence.*
- Woman as Temptress. *Temptations arise which will distract the hero from their journey.*
- Atonement with the father. *Initiation with that which holds power in the hero's life. It is usually in the form of a father figure who has the power of life and death.*
- Apotheosis. *The death of the old self/the transformation part/moves beyond and takes a period of rest.*
- The Ultimate Boon (reward). *The boon is the reward and marks the attainment of the goal like a gold medal in the Olympics.*

RETURN

- Refusal of the Return. *After finding bliss, the hero does not want to return.*
- The Magic Flight. *The hero has to escape with the item they have been searching for.*
- Rescue from Without. *Assistance from a wise person enables the hero to escape.*
- The Crossing of the Return Threshold. *The hero must return to the world to complete the quest.*
- Master of the Two Worlds. *This is when the hero transcends two worlds, like Neo in the Matrix.*

- Freedom to live. *The master has now changed and returns to society with an insight to share. Since they have faced death, they now have the freedom to live. They live in the moment without regret for the past. They often have transcended life.*

Consider the above structure in terms of film: The Matrix, Star Wars and The Shawshank Redemption.

All of the above are based on the specific three act structure; however, with all this in mind, the audience now anticipates such structure. It has become standard, predictable and a little dull. The challenge is to know the structure but tailor it to your story - your way. Try not to be too predictable/clichéd.

In terms of books, take a look at Sophie's World, Lord of The Rings, The Beach, The life of Pi, and The Alchemist. All of these books embody the above structural arrangements. There are endless books that apply the above structure and after a while you will automatically notice the sequences. When you are aware of the standard literary construction, it can ruin the reading experience. Although, there are books by authors like W.G. Seabald—Rings of Saturn who tenuously links thoughts and delves into alternative approaches to linking events.

Once you have made the mind map, consider your own specific event arrangement. Take what you have created and place them in a linear timeline. Once you have created an order you are happy with, write a sentence about what is happening to enable yourself clarity of thought and an understanding of what you have arranged. Now you have the basic structure for the story/script/or anything you fancy!

CHAPTER 11

Narrative – The Seven Stories

Consider the fact that our world is immersed in stories. There are stories in newspapers, books, magazines, theatre, film and even our lives are re-accounted as stories. Have you ever wondered why that is? Why do we all love stories? Why do we never question what it is about story that we find so fascinating? From our earliest age, we demand that story after story is fed to us and we sit, listen and absorb. Throughout history, storytellers have taken pride of place around fires. They have fascinated tribes, villagers and noblemen. So what exactly makes us desire the story experience?

From a different perspective-consider the act of reading. How can words conjure stories in our mind? How does that series of words stimulate an internal film?

With a world full of stories, it may be surprising to discover there are seven basic narrative types. Obviously there are anomalies and some stories that encompass more than one story type are listed below:

The seven basic plots by Christopher Booker discuss in-depth the seven story types.

The seven types of story:

1) Overcoming the monster/the thrilling escape from death.
   Consider the stories of Gilgamesh, Beowulf, Greek Mythology, Norse Sagas, St. George and the Dragon, Jaws, Dracula, King Kong, Godzilla and War of the Worlds.
   The monster represents our darkest fears. It is usually a predator; it protects a treasure and is an obstacle on the hero's path. When confronted, the monster becomes an avenger—it is vicious. The 'monster' theme also turns up in war stories, westerns, thrillers and some science fiction.

2) Rags to Riches
   Cinderella, The Ugly Duckling, King Arthur, David Copperfield, Jane Eyre and Slum Dog Millionaire are just a few examples. The essence of the story is that a person bought up in poverty, who is usually persecuted by dark authority figures, enters an adventure, which leads them to dazzling splendour. The result is that those who mistreated them in the first place have the tables turned and gaze upon them in adoration. The more modern version of this story takes the form of a person living in mundane circumstances in hope of achieving their fortune. This usually means that they go to an unknown city. They then move through the narrative learning and failing but finally end up with great success. They

return to their original circumstances, new, wealthy and changed.

3) The Quest
   Lord of The Rings, Odysseus, Raiders of the Lost Ark, The Hobbit, Watership Down and Pilgrim's Progress.

   The quest pulls the hero to some distant, all-important goal. It follows the structure of the call, the journey, the ordeals that lead to frustration, the final ordeals and the reward. There is usually a thrilling escape from death. The hero then returns 'home' with the treasure/reward.

4) Voyage and Return
   Alice In Wonderland, Goldilocks, The Lion, the Witch and the Wardrobe, The Wizard of Oz, Tom's Midnight Garden and The Time Machine (H.G Wells). A group of characters or an individual character travels outside of their everyday usual surroundings into another world completely cut off from the first. In the second world, everything is disconcertingly abnormal. At first, the discovery of the world is exciting but over time they start to feel trapped or stuck. Shadowy characters appear and threaten the hero who feels increasingly trapped. They usually make a thrilling escape to return to normality, which they now appreciate. They return to their reality new, changed and appreciative.

5) Comedy

The Comedy of Errors, Bridget Jones, Shopaholic, The Taming of he Shrew. Originally, a comedy was not intended purely for laughs; the narrative revealed a character's self-delusion. The character was usually blinded by their own egotism. In addition, the reader/audience is aware that they can see something that the character cannot. It is the contradiction of how the character interprets the world around them – take for example they believe they are organised but everything surrounding them is scattered and disorganised. The narrative considers a hero, who has traits that they are unaware of, taking a journey to become more aware through the humorous circumstances they encounter. The hero, in this instance, could be considered a baddy who plans something malicious but the situations they encounter ruin the plan. There are dark shadowy characters who enable conflict but it is often circumstantial and funny. In a modern comedy, all the characters are brought to light and reconciled to create a world that is united.

6) Tragedy

Bonny and Clyde, Hamlet, Thelma and Louise, Million Dollar Baby and Carmen.

The tragedy follows a similar structure to the other stories: The anticipation stage where the hero/heroin feels incomplete and live in mundanity. They have a problem they need to solve. This results in a course of action which takes them on a journey to achieve their goals. Things go wrong, obstacles appear and they lose control. A series of circumstances drive the characters to the extreme and a choice is offered... This is where the tragedy is different to the other stories; the outcome is death, destruction or a death wish.

7) Rebirth

The Secret Garden, Snow White and Sleeping Beauty.

This story enables the hero/heroin a journey of self-realisation. The enemy comes from within. The story begins with the hero/heroin being someway incomplete. They then encounter a dark power, that dark power remains dominant throughout the story until there is a confrontation between the hero and the dark power. The result of the conflict is that the hero or heroin end up imprisoned in a state of living death. Miraculous redemption-a situation occurs where the hero or heroin are liberated from the state and become whole.

CHAPTER 12

Hooks Lines and Stinkers!

When reading a book, which five things make you want to read on?

What is it that captures your attention when reading a story?

How far will you read before you get bored?

What is it that makes you stop?

The hook is an opening line or paragraph that provides the reader with the incentive to read on. It is often insightful and provides a hint at the theme within the book.

Look at the following examples:

- A squat grey building of only thirty four storeys. Over the main entrance the words,

CENTRAL LONDON HATCHERY AND CONDITIONING CENTRE, and in a shield the world state's motto:

COMMUNITY, IDENTITY, STABILITY.

(Aldus Huxley - Brave New World)

- Ours is a tragic age so we refuse to take it tragically. (D.H Lawrence – Lady Chatterley's lover).

- It is a truth universally acknowledged, that a single man in the possession of a good fortune, must be in want of a wife. (Jane Austin)
- It was a bright cold day in April, and the clocks were striking thirteen. (1984 George Orwell)
- No one would believe in the last years of the nineteenth century, the world was being watched keenly and closely by intelligences greater than man. (War of the Worlds – H.G Wells).

The above are a few classic examples of how a theme and a question is set to the reader.

There are numerous hooking strategies. Consider the following and how you can apply these techniques:

- Send the reader straight into the heart of a conflict or difficult situation. Try a powerful controversy between two contrasting characters.
- Consider a difficult situation set up which begs the question how do they escape? This could be used to set the story and then we introduce the character in their 'mundane world.'
- The opening does not have to slap you – a situation or a way of speaking could be mysterious or suggestive.

Consider the opening of films – in Bourne Identity a body floats in the middle of the ocean. The scene can be set, a question raised and then we can move to a contrasting situation. If, for example, we apply this to a simple conversation, the conversation could reveal something but when you are about to make a discovery, the confession or conversation is interrupted or the subject is changed.

The way that I look at this, is that you are intending to seduce your reader (through literary skill), you must offer a 'narrative promise'. This will give the reader the incentive to continue reading. The desire to find out is a great driving force. For me, the mystery is the hint, the suggestion or the provocation. You are offering a reward in partaking in the reading of your writing.

One little tip, go through the bestsellers and look at their opening lines, or stand in a book shop and work your way along the shelf. Ask yourself what works and what does not work.

With all this in mind, personally I like to begin each chapter with a hook and end the chapter with a teaser/closer. Each teaser drives the reader to want to find out more. Questions need to be answered, but they are answered when the reader is not expecting it. I personally like the thought of when the reader puts the book down they go away and try and figure out what is happening. Using this technique, I purposely alter the pacing and play with suspense. I build questions through the chapters which are answered in the following chapters but then provide more questions that will be answered further on in the book. The way that I do this is not to give too much away. When I plot my chapters I consider questions that I want raised early on and pace the answers throughout the book. This is purposeful and takes time but there is great satisfaction in it. I often have a theme and a series of questions that I intend to answer by writing the book.

CHAPTER 13

Character Limitations, Conflict and Emotion

As your characters develop you will begin to notice that they have certain ways of dealing with things. How the character responds to a situation reveals an enormous amount about who they 'really' are. Their behaviour is the result of choices, based on inner beliefs/inner world, which results in the action/response. In essence, how a character behaves in a situation is the result of a combination of inner world beliefs, external influences such as environment and society. The resultant behaviour has followed a complex process that has travelled through thought patterns, past references and comparative situations. With all this in mind, to reveal more about the character we need to push them to their limits and beyond! Hoorah!

Conflict

When we reference conflict we are not just referring to obstacles or arguing. Instead there are other such conflicts such as loyalty, personal dilemmas, lies and confrontation.

Outer conflicts are situations that obstruct the character from achieving their goals.

- Argument/disagreement
- Hostile encounter – battle, war, domestic

- Clash between two parties – this could be a business deal, landlord and tenant, neighbours, competitive teams
- Contradictory ideals/opposition
- Facing a 'monster'
- Imprisonment/trapped/stuck
- The action of making an actual change in their life

The second phase of outer conflict is when the character conflicts with the environment surrounding them. This could be nature, society or the universe.

- Natural disaster, weather, volcanos, tornados, tsunami and mud slides
- Invasion of external forces—asteroids, birds, locusts and disease
- Social environment

Inner conflict – this is based on inner beliefs and self-worth. There is a struggle against self-imposed limitations. Often the character discovers a new way to perceive the world which involves having to go against an old way of doing things. The inner conflict often takes place when this shift occurs and externally everything that they knew as 'right' falls away. Essentially the character is locked in a conflict against the 'self'.

- Incorrect or new beliefs
- Facing fears
- Discovering parts of 'self' they never knew they had

- Ethical decision
- Betrayal
- Emotions they have never experienced.

When considering conflicts, you may be interested in the psychological theory of projection. What we do not like in others are parts of ourselves that we project onto others. We can only recognise behaviours that we know or understand. So for example what the character has to overcome is 'mirrored' in the qualities of the baddy. By the character overcoming the baddy they are in actual fact conquering the part of the self they denied (metaphorically). By doing this the character achieves character growth, acceptance and integration.

With this in mind, in relation to your structure and middle section of your structure/second act, consider the qualities that you would like your character develop through external conflict and internal conflict.

Here is a little exercise to enable you to develop some ideas on how to push your character to the limits:

Imagine a series of no win situations, how can you take your character into such situations? How will they react?

What is the worst moral dilemma you could force your character to confront?

What dark secret could they discover/have to deal with/witness?

What part of themselves have they completely denied that they are going to have to face?

The character witnesses a situation. What is this situation and what is the result of sharing it?

Pushing your character to the limit – this is your opportunity to almost break them. By doing this you are able to understand your character and provide the reader with the opportunity to experience the situation from an entirely new perspective whether it is emotional, physical or a combination of both. Actually you also get to experience and push yourself too! Brilliant!!!

To push the character to the limits you may consider the following obstacles:

- Physical obstacles come in the form of mountains, rivers to cross, creatures to escape
- Other characters enable conflict, confrontation, emotion and reaction
- Mental obstacles come in the form of 'how' do we put this idea into action
- Belief systems that obstruct such as 'big men don't cry' or that it is wrong to show emotion
- Cultural obstacles – how the system, faith, social belief, social hierarchy restricts those within it
- Supernatural forces to overcome
- Time limitations where there is a count down or a time limit in which the adventure should be completed

Ultimately, obstacles provide opportunity for the character to grow and transform. The more difficult the obstacles, the more they learn and the more we learn about them. What's more, the character extends their comfort zone and faces fears. During the process, we, the readers, are able to have an insight into their inner worlds by how each obstacle is approached. Do they approach differently? Throughout your write the obstacles should slowly become more difficult and more challenging.

CHAPTER 14

Editing / Proofreading and Emotion

First things first – what makes you want to read a book or an article? What is it that makes you spend your valuable time mentally digesting someone else's words? What would capture the attention of your reader and direct them to read your written works? With all this in mind – how do you make this writing the best that it can be?

Your end goal for your writing may not be for the world to read it; however, once you have written something that you feel is worthwhile then why not share? You have the opportunity to give the world an insight into your unique perspective using your talent. As long as you have enjoyed the journey of creation - then why not?

What I will say is before you share make sure you have edited, re-edited and proofed your work. There will come a time when you will 'feel' ready to share. Until you have this feeling do not make some of these common mistakes:

- Sending out a few chapters when the whole book is not written.
  Imagine an editor says yes and asks you to send the whole lot in... Ooops!
- Sending out half-baked works – meaning you have the basics of a draft but no finalisation.
  I admit this – I did this once and it lost me the deal!
- Sending out an idea without any actual story.

I heard this at a writer's conference. It annoys editors and agents! In their words – it makes them bristle!

- The writing draft not being in one tense or from a multitude of perspectives.
Again, at a writing conference they said that since time is limited, and publishers are under pressure, they do not have the time or the inclination to re-write your work. They can tweak but gone are the days where an editor will completely re-write.

Editing:
How I see editing is the re-organisation of the book to make the narrative the best it can be. I consider its coherence, its order and fill in additional parts that make the writing 'whole'. The second part of the edit for me is finding the best way to write what I want to say. In the first draft, you provide a sketch of the idea – now you decorate it, embellish it and make it slap! Yipeeeee for that!

With the above in mind, I have learned to approach writing is as follows:
- There is no rush. Complete the draft, put it away and write something else. Your writing will continue to improve – it is like exercise – you gradually build the writing muscle.
- After a few months (honestly – no less) print out the whole thing and have a read through – do not use a pen yet but write notes on a separate pad with the page numbers. Note what is missing, what does not

make sense, what can be removed or added. You just need to read and absorb the whole thing before chopping it up!

- Keep the first version saved in its entirety as version one.
- For version two, go through the whole book on the computer and organise according to your notes. Ask yourself is it coherent – can a reader follow it?

First re-write

- Can the reader understand the story – is it coherent and in order?
- Is this story as dramatic and interesting as it can be?
- Is there anything that the audience needs to know to make it clearer?
- Do my characters have a tendency to do things that fall out of their natural characteristics?
- Is the structure the best it can be? Can I make it more effective? Rather than stay with the three act structure, would a five act structure work better?
- Is my point of entry dramatic enough?
- Whose story am I telling and am I telling it from the best point of view? An audience/reader has a short attention span. Constant switching between perspectives or points of view is annoying. With a number of perspectives, the best thing to do is make it from the omnipresent point of view where everything can be viewed.
- Now ask what is original about this story? How can I make it unique? What is the selling point?

- What is its dramatic structure? Consider both the overall structure and the contributing structures.
- What are the surprises, quirks, twists and turns? Make them fun. Predictability loses interest!
- What can you hold back or have you held back from the reader to be revealed only when they need to know?
- Is it the right length?
- What is the message/theme? Have you stuck to it?
- Why did you write the story? Who do you intend to share it with? Does it fulfil these needs?

Structure:

Act I – have you introduced the characters effectively and set the tone and style?

What are the critical elements? Have you clearly demonstrated a crisis point? Have you enabled audience identification?

Potential issues: lack of clarity or understanding of the character goal, motivation or personality.

Act II – have you taken the characters through obstacles, raised the stakes and pushed them to their limits? Have they moved past the points of no return? This section needs to drive the reader and inspire through identification.

The potential downfalls of this act is that it lacks direction, drawn out and is too obvious. The characters do not engage either.

Act III

The whole purpose of act three is to enable resolution, all the parts of the character, the structure and the narrative are united here and come to a clear resolution. Every loose end needs to be tied so that the reader experiences completion. The dangers in this section are that questions are not answered and the reader goes away feeling dissatisfied.

Openings and Chapter Closers:

Have you written the best opening?

Is your point of entry exciting and enticing enough? This is for all chapters and all acts within the narrative.

Have you raised enough questions? Have you given the reader the incentive to continue?

Is the visual setting interesting?

Is there conflict? Is there enough internal and external conflict? Is anything happening?

Do you know the protagonist and what they want?

Do you want to turn pages?

Each scene/chapter will end - have you effectively ended and driven the reader to continue?

If not how can you do this? What needs to be made better?

Character/Dialogue Re-write:

Do I need all these characters? Are there any more characters that I need? Are there any that I can get rid of?

One of the main issues in story is that there are too many characters and they are not definite. It is like the reader has to stand in a crowd. What is even worse is when the characters just sound the same. Are the characters individual? Have they got a way of speaking that can be identified to them?

Are the conversations authentic and not staid?

What do the conversations reveal about the characters and how do they drive the story forwards?

Sometimes a character has simply been invented to drive the story – is there a better way of moving the story forwards?

Transformative Arc

How does each character change or evolve? Does this tie in with your original intention for the character?

Have all characters experienced a variety of emotion or experienced parts of themselves that they did not know existed?

What changes do they experience and at what point do they experience these changes?

Are the character's emotions defined from the outset with a demonstration of how they respond externally to these emotions?

Are you character's values challenged at crisis points? What changes?

Consider the character's attitude, behaviour, distinctive habits. How do these tie in with the way they look, dress and present themselves?

Consider surprise responses that demonstrate a change in the character.

With regards to their motivation, how do we make it mysterious? How can we generate additional interest in what the character is using to drive them? Can the reader figure it out? Unpredictability and the unexpected in terms of behaviour are rather interesting to utilize as a tool.

Avoid stereotypes and cliché – it is boring.

Dialogue

Keep dialogue lively, progressive and flowing. Avoid conversation which enable yes and no answers. This will cause the flow to come to a standstill! Attempt to keep the dialogue in an exchange.

When dialogue rambles and lacks direction the reader's mind will wander! FACT! Say what needs to be said!

Where is the spark? Where is the emotion or the 'play'?

Could you remove some dialogue and suggest the same through action?

Emotion

Feel the emotion and write the emotion. Have you felt the emotion throughout the writing? Can you make it clearer? Can you make the reader cry, laugh, angry or experience sadness. Boredom is not one you want the reader to experience!

CHAPTER 15

Endings, Synopsis and Selling.

Endings and beginnings are best when they leave a positive mental impression or question. If your reader wants more then you have succeeded. Yipeee!!!! If your reader leaves feeling dissatisfied, the word of mouth will simply be a bitter taste in the mouth.

Personally, when I read a book, I like everything to tie up, come together and have a sense of resolution. I like to feel satisfied. Think of all the books where you have come away satisfied and those which have not worked. What is the difference?

Types of Ending:

Hollywood

The happy ending where everyone lives happily ever after. The boy gets the girl, the girl gets shoes and there is probably some fluffy, white puppy involved. Oh and not to mention, peace comes to the planet and everyone has exceptional dentistry! I sometimes refer to this as cheese-mongering! Examples of this are pretty much the majority of Hollywood films – hence Hollywood ending!

Ironic Ending

The bittersweet ending whereby the hero wins through loss. Candide by Voltaire, the theme is that everything happens for the best; however the irony is that the characters are united in love when they are old and physically diseased.

The Tragic Ending

The hero loses and the antagonist wins, or they both die. Even though the conflict is resolved at the hero's sacrifice/expense, the point of the story is confirmed. This is very much a Thelma and Louise example.

Surprise Ending

The surprise lies in a twist, a revelation or something completely unexpected. This then changes the understanding of the story trajectory/outcome. When this is skilfully written, this is the best ending that you can have! Consider Sixth Sense when Bruce Willis is actually the ghost.

Vague or Undefined Ending

This is when the story is left open-ended. The reader is left to imagine the outcome or what could happen. To be honest this type of ending is infuriating! Remember when you have spent the time reading an entire book to arrive at an ending which says – imagine what could happen now... (Grrrrrrrrrrrrrrrr!!!!!!!!!!) Horror films usually use this ending so that the audience can go away to imagine the worst that can happen.

Endings

Is your final ending satisfying? Have you taken your reader on a journey to actually show them something they would not have expected? Try writing three alternative endings... Find a twist – find a new direction and step beyond the illusion of obviousness. This is the challenge and a secret satisfaction. Is everything united? Write a list of what needs to be united... Are you satisfied? Will the reader be satisfied? What will the reader take away from reading this work? Can it be better?

What if you are going to write a sequel or a series of books? Well the ending has to make the reader want to buy the next book. Quite often there is a question set up that will bug the reader or the ending will create a resolution and a new beginning. Take for instance at the end of a journey the character realises there is a further journey to discover more. Imagine a character finds their long-lost sibling only to discover there are three more that they never knew existed. The ending has to drive the reader to want to read more or find out more and it needs to be suggested at the end of the book to intrigue the reader enough for them to actively find the next book.

Polish!!!!!!!!!!!!!!!!!!!!!!

By this point you have made every check... It might be worth creating a checklist. Now that you know everything is present, it is time to refine and make the writing the best it can be. Is the style the same all the way through? Is the voice the same? Is the writing fluid? Read it aloud and feel a pleasure hearing those words that you created. One way to really hear what you have written is read aloud into your phone and record it. Play it back and see if anything else needs to be filled out/embellished or cut.

Finally and this is a biggy – ask an honest friend to give you feedback. When I say honest – I mean a brutal friend. No one wants to hurt your feelings but sometimes you need the slap... You usually know what is missing but you have been denying it. Now is the time to test your work and see if it is ready for the wider world!

Time to start marketing and making people aware of your work

Theme

Informing the audience of the complete story of your book in one sentence is certainly a skill in itself. Imagine all those years of work simply being in one sentence. All that possibility and thought in one sentence... Is it possible? Of course it is...

To be honest – this took quite a time for me to get my head around this. The moment you meet a journalist – you have to be able to say something like the below:

The Ocean Callings is a teenage story about love, death and the heart connection set in Gardenstown, Scotland.

Labyrinthine asks questions about art, synchronicity and the divine from the perspective of a broken eccentric artist.

Goylegate – One Gargantuan adventure is a children's story about a girl with limited memory attempting to stop world annihilation by the vengeful Chimera.

How to break it down:

- What is your theme?
- What are the key points of the story?
- What adjectives best describe what you do?
- Bear in mind that you need to incorporate the who, the what, the where and possibly the how.

The synopsis:

Slap! Whack! Crack! The key to a synopsis is to grab your reader's attention from the first line. Agents, editors and producers receive hundreds of synopsis per week – so make yours grab them by the throat! You have all mastered the art of the hook – now bring this into the synopsis. The synopsis will set the tone of your writing and will reveal your skills at writing and communicating the story. The whole point of the synopsis is to tell the reader what the book is about and not how things happen.

A good synopsis will:

- Be written in present tense
- Provide insight into the basic story idea
- It will enable the reader to imagine the project from beginning to end
- It will also provide the location, mood, period genre and journey

- Contain only 'active' sentences without passive voice
- There will be some enticing questions

Before you go any further, research the market and see if anything similar is out there? How did they approach it? In terms of publishers and editors, make sure they represent the genre you are writing. Consider whether you could reference a similar book on their list.

Make a list of the key plot points:

- What is it that your reader wants to know?
- This simply needs to be a basic but it enables elaboration further into the body of the writing.
- It does not need to detail sub-plots or lesser characters.
- Ask yourself what are the key things within this story and what does the main character experience?
- What are the key turning points?
- What is the character's motivation and goal?
- All of this should be written in simple, fast paced sentences to enable fast and fluid reading.
- When writing the synopsis consider the showing and not telling.
- Do not ask too many empty questions. However do bring in some questions. Create mystery and intrigue.
- When it is ready, leave it to brew for two days and go back with fresh eyes. Proofread, tidy and finalise.

Again it might be worth reading it aloud and recording it.

The Test:

- Does the synopsis enable the reader story clarity? Could they convey your story concept to others?
- Can an idiot understand your synopsis? Do they instantly know what it is about?
- Is it an honest portrayal of the story?
- Could it be better?
- When the synopsis is ready, give it to an objective party and ask 'would you be tempted to read the entire novel after reading the synopsis?' If the answer is no – ask why and re-write.
- Search for book and film synopsis online and read them until you find one which you feel is outstanding. Note what makes it leap out and then emulate.

<u>**Selling and Promotion**</u>

There are two ways you can do this but either way, at some point you will be involved in promotion.

Doing it your own way:

What makes you buy a book? Most people buy because of the cover. Make an interesting cover or find someone that can. There are millions of books out there, so make a concerted effort to visually hook your reader.

- Amazon Digital Platform. It will sell your work on Kindle and Amazon.
- Createspace make print on demand books and will sell them on your behalf on Amazon.
- If you look at Smashwords – they will sell to Sony, Ipad and they have their own e-books.
- Blurb – self publish.
- Lightening Source – print on demand.
- Lulu.com – you can put your books together on this to get an idea of how it looks.
  Resources:
- Writer's and Artists Handbook.
- Society of Children's Book Authors and Illustrators.
- The Writer's Market is an American journal of all international markets for magazines, publishers and literary agents.

Blogging :

How will people find you and know you exist? Blogging is one of the best things that you can do – you can publicise your blog through Facebook and Twitter. How about when you finish your book release it chapter by chapter and post on your Facebook page. State you are going to publish the first ten chapters. WordPress and Blogspot are two of the major places for posting blogs. Alternatively build your own website and blog there. Once your work is on Amazon you can create an author page and your blogs and tweets from Twitter can directly feed that.

Have a look at your favourite authors and see how they promote.

Now is the beginning of your writing journey... You have the tools – now build something brilliant!!!!

The old school way:

Take the Writer's and Artist's Handbook and write a list of all the agents that represent books in your genre. Put a covering letter, synopsis and first three chapters together. Follow their submission guidelines and then wait... and wait...

Being that many of my students are impatient and wanted to get their books out to the world as fast as they could, most went for the self-publishing route. In doing so, they experienced a journey and built a network of people who they could use as proof-readers and editors. Most found that they liked to have control of what they created. The counter argument for going the classic way is that once you are accepted by a publisher you have the best people in the industry to support you. The only real issue is the time involved. If you want to write for pleasure and then share, I would go the self-publish route. Also, bear in mind, you can send out your work to agents and publishers whilst establishing your books on line. The choice is yours and the way you choose will result in a published book. That is the joy of it.

CHAPTER 16

Writing as Healing

Just a little bit more… Since writing this book I have been asked about writing as healing and catharsis.

I realised there are a few little exercises that need to be shared that can be used for healing, resolution or catharsis. Quite often when we are in situations we are unable to fully process them because we are 'in it'. So I suggested some of my students use free writing and an objective viewpoint to resolve situations. The free writing enables you to make contact with your unconscious and bypass the conscious thinking area. So for example sometimes we feel 'stuck' in life and what we could do is use a character with similar traits to ourselves and put them in the 'stuck' situation and write them out of it.

For example 'a character feels it is time to end a relationship; however, the other partner is reliant on them.' Start the writing with 'When (NAME OF CHARACTER) decided to end their relationship they…. (from this moment you free-write until nothing is left.)

In addition, you can use this technique to discover what you really want to do with your life. Try the following prompt to surprise yourself: If (YOUR NAME) had a year to really live life to the full they would…. (free-write your little heart out). Bear in mind there are no limits on what you can write – just let it go and figure out the how later.

Another great prompt to resolve a situation:

The best thing that can be done about NAME THE SITUATION is... (free-write until it is out of your system).

This technique is also good for emotion and processing emotions. Again, sometimes it is better to write objectively. Try this:

NAME OF PERSON/YOUR NAME/CHARACTER NAME (pick one) is feeling WRITE THE EMOTION about SITUATION because....

With this one you can use your own situation or situation you can see developing. It can help you gain a perspective on the people involved by writing their name instead of yours. Alternatively you can use a character's name to completely remove yourself.

My final healing prompt is this 'To be the ultimate me I would be.... And all I need to change is... How I want to approach this is...' This one provides a huge insight into personal growth and the path towards it.

Everything that is written in this book is just a guide and you will find that through writing you will find your own way, an easy way. Once you find your system repeat it and enjoy it. What you may find is that you will be in a rush to complete a book, but in all truth, completion and releasing it is not half as fun as writing the book. As clichéd as it is – the journey is a fantastic one where you and your characters overcome obstacles and find solutions to some quite ridiculous problems. My advice is don't rush, enjoy and create quality. Enjoy the journey and I hope you find great joy in what you create.

Fiction Titles by Ruby Allure:

Labyrinthine

The Ocean Callings

Money Farm

Love Hunt I – Dating

Love Hunt II – The Love Game

Goylegate – One Gargantuan Scandal!

Clan Destine

The Office Zoo – A Field Guide to Office Animal Observation